Luis Walter Álvarez

by Tina Randall

Raintree

Chicago, Illinois

For information, address the publisher:
Raintree, 100 N. LaSalle, Suite 1200, Chicago, IL 60602

Printed and bound in China by South China Printing Company.
07 06 05
10 9 8 7 6 5 4 3 2 1

Library of Congress Cataloging-in-Publication Data:

Randall, Tina.
  Luis Walter Álvarez / Tina Randall.
      p. cm. –- (Hispanic-American biographies)
  Includes bibliographical references and index.
  ISBN 1-4109-1295-7 (hc) –- ISBN 1-4109-1303-1 (pbk.)
  1. Álvarez, Luis W., 1911–-Juvenile literature. 2. Physicists–-United States–-Biography–-Juvenile literature. I.
Title. II. Series.
  QC16.A48R36 2005
  530'.092–-dc22

                                        2004025313

Acknowledgments
The publisher would like to thank the following for permission to reproduce photographs:
p.4, KPA/Zuma Press; pp. 7, 15, 16, 19, 28, 29, 36 Corbis/Bettman; pp.8, 20, 23, 40, 43, 44, 46, 53, 57, 59 Ernest
Orlando Lawrence Berkeley National Laboratory; p.13 Lonely Planet Images/Raymond Hillstrom; p.24 Corbis/Hulton-
Deutsch Collection; p.39 AP Wide World Photo/Stanley Troutman; p.48 Newscom/Zuma Photos; p.55 Corbis/Roger
Ressmeyer.

Cover photograph: Ernest Orlando Lawrence Berkeley National Laboratory

Every effort has been made to contact copyright holders of any material reproduced in this book. Any omissions will
be rectified in subsequent printings if notice is given to the publisher.

Some words are shown in bold, **like this**. You can find out what
they mean by looking in the glossary.

Contents

Luis Walter Álvarez was an important physicist during the twentieth century.

Introduction

Luis Walter Álvarez was a famous scientist who made important discoveries in **physics**. He studied **atoms**, which are the basic building blocks of everything that exists in our world. Because of his work, Álvarez was awarded the **Nobel Prize** in 1968. He received this important honor for discovering better ways of identifying the tiny things that form atoms, called subatomic particles. He invented machines that are used to study atoms and the particles that form them. Can you imagine that? Not only did he work with atoms, which for a long time were believed to be the smallest things in the universe, he actually discovered ways to study the even smaller pieces that form atoms!

Luis Álvarez was interested in many different things. His curiosity and interests went from the world of invisible particles to the light of the stars and astronomy, and how they relate to life on Earth. An important hobby of his was investigating why dinosaurs became extinct. He even went on archeological expeditions with his son to learn more about it.

Álvarez did most of his work in physics at the University of California at Berkeley and at the Lawrence Radiation Laboratory. But during World War II, the U.S. government needed his help, and he went to the Massachusetts Institute of Technology (MIT) to work. Later, he joined the team that developed the **atomic bomb**. Álvarez witnessed the dropping of the two atomic bombs on Japan at the end of World War II. He was able to see the effect of **nuclear weapons** first-hand, and realized that they would change the world forever.

Although Álvarez was worried about the destructive power of the atomic bomb, he was also convinced that it made the war end sooner and, as a result, saved lives. After having seen the bomb dropped over Japan, he wrote a letter to his son Walter, who was only a little boy at the time. In that letter, Álvarez tells his son that although he feels sad about having been part of creating something as destructive as the atomic bomb, he also feels hope that it will bring the countries of the world together and prevent future wars.

He said, "Alfred Nobel—the man who left his money to be used to give prizes to people who did great things in science, literature and peace—thought that his invention of high explosives . . . [would make] wars too terrible, but unfortunately it had just the opposite reaction. Our new destructive force is so many thousands of times worse that it may make Nobel's dream come true."

This is a picture of the Enola Gay, *the plane that dropped the atomic bomb on Hiroshima, Japan.* Álvarez *rode in an airplane that followed the* Enola Gay, *and witnessed the destruction of the atomic bomb firsthand.*

Some people think that the creation of the atomic bomb was bad for science and for future scientific discoveries. However, Álvarez was always very interested in learning about our world and he accomplished many things. His inventions and discoveries are an inspiration for everyone, and remind us that we need to always ask questions about science and the future.

This is a photograph of Álvarez at his lab in Berkeley, California in 1966.

Chapter 1:
Family Roots in Knowledge and Service

Luis Walter Álvarez was born on June 13, 1911. His family was always interested in learning. This dedication motivated Luis to try to understand the world better even when he was very young.

Luis's family had a **diverse** cultural background, with both Hispanic and Irish heritage. His grandfather on his father's side was a native of Spain who moved to Cuba and then to the United States, where he settled in California. Luis's grandfather became successful in the real estate business and later studied at medical school. He then moved his family to Hawaii, where he worked as a doctor.

Luis's mother's family was originally from Ireland. They moved to Foochow, China, where they founded a missionary school. Luis's mother went to that school and then moved to California, where she finished high school and then went to college in Berkeley.

Luis's father and mother, Walter and Harriet, met when they were studying at the university in Berkeley. Their excitement about learning new things made it easy for Álvarez to love learning as well. For Álvarez, this love became an adventure that lasted all his life.

Luis's father, Walter C. Álvarez, was a doctor who had his own office. He was also a medical **researcher**. A researcher is someone who studies and does experiments to learn new things about a certain subject. Learning was also very important to Álvarez's mother, Harriet. She was an elementary school teacher, and taught Luis at home until he was in third grade. As a young child, Luis wasn't very healthy, so he could not go to school like most kids do.

Luis's parents' desire to learn and use their knowledge to help everyone around them was a strong influence on all of the children in the Álvarez family. Luis had an older sister named Gladys, a younger brother named Bob, and a younger sister named Bernice. Walter and Harriet set an example for their children and encouraged them to follow their dreams.

Álvarez's earliest interests in science and technology were encouraged by his father when he was a young boy and during his high school years in California. By the time he was ten years old, Luis knew how to use mechanical tools in his father's workshop, and he also had a basic understanding of electricity. When he was only eleven years old, he and his father built a radio together.

Luis Álvarez loved the outdoors and adventures. One time his father took him and his brother Bob to go rock climbing. During this adventure, Luis and Bob were caught in a rock and ice slide. To escape a dangerous fall, Luis dug into the ice with his axe and held on until the ice and rock slide was over. Afterward, Luis read about what you should do to stay safe in rock slides, and he realized that he had narrowly escaped death. He had held onto the axe in a way that wasn't very safe. From this experience, Luis learned that being daring isn't the only thing you need if you want to have exciting new experiences and discover new things. It is just as important to know how to be safe and to do things carefully.

The Early Education of a Physicist

Luis went to elementary school in San Francisco and then to the city's Polytechnic High School. This was a special school for students with very good mechanical skills. Here Álvarez also took classes to prepare for college. Then his father took a job as a researcher with the Mayo Clinic, and the family moved to Rochester, Minnesota. Luis had a lot of fun during these years. He made friends with boys and girls, spent time ice skating, visited friends' houses after school, and enjoyed ballroom dancing, which he had learned in San Francisco. However, Luis's high school classes in science weren't challenging enough for him. Since he was so interested in science, his dad hired a science tutor for him. A tutor is a teacher who works with a student one-on-one. The work was slow and difficult, but Luis worked hard and everything he learned helped him succeed later on.

During high school, Luis worked at the Mayo Clinic one summer. This experience helped him learn how we can use what we learn in science classes. Luis learned how to do experiments and create devices using tools in the laboratory.

In 1928, Luis Álvarez enrolled at the University of Chicago to study chemistry. Then during his junior year, he learned about **optics**, which is the study of light, in a course he was taking. To study optics, you need to study physics, too, so Álvarez decided to change his main course of studies to physics. He said that the study of light was "love at first sight."

Álvarez decided to continue his studies in physics and become a true expert in the field. He was lucky to study and work with the best scientists at the school, including Arthur Compton, who had won the Nobel Prize. Compton gave Álvarez advice and encouraged him to work on his own.

Álvarez began his college career at the University of Chicago, one of the top universities in the United States.

One of the most important things that Álvarez learned during his years at the university is that you shouldn't be satisfied only with what you learn in the classroom. You can also teach yourself about many subjects by reading library books. Librarians and teachers can help you find good books, and, like Álvarez, you can learn more about the things that fascinate you.

Looking at the World from Above

Luis Álvarez described himself as someone who was **resourceful** and confident, so it's not surprising that one of his favorite hobbies was flying airplanes. He learned to fly a plane by himself after only three hours of instruction!

Álvarez enjoyed flying all his life. He once wrote: "Heroes have been important to my development as a scientist . . . In **aviation**, my two principal heroes are Jimmy Doolittle and Chuck Yeager." Jimmy Doolittle flew bomber planes during World War II, and Chuck Yeager was the first pilot to fly faster than the speed of sound.

Heroes were Álvarez's inspiration in both the research lab and in the skies. He never limited his possibilities to learn or his admiration for the people who had something to teach him. Álvarez had many opportunities to learn during his years at the University of Chicago. Once he became interested in optics and light, he studied them with great enthusiasm.

Jimmy Doolittle was a famous pilot during World War II.

In 1932, Álvarez published his first paper in a scientific journal. When scientists make discoveries or do important research, they often write articles about their work and publish them in magazines called journals. Álvarez's paper discussed how he had discovered a way to measure light. He used simple tools such as a broken phonograph record, a light bulb, and a yard stick to discover how white light could be bounced off the surface of the record and be broken into the "rainbow colors." This would be one of many experiments that would lead Álvarez to make important scientific discoveries.

Álvarez spent much of his time in laboratories making important discoveries.

Chapter 2:
Finding a Career

Just after Álvarez finished his advanced studies at the University of Chicago, he married Geraldine Smithwick, a student in her final year at the university. Álvarez and Geraldine had two children, Walter and Jean. His son Walter also liked science and grew up to become a **geologist**. Geologists study rocks and the history of the earth. Luis Álvarez and his son later worked together to understand why dinosaurs became **extinct**.

While he was still in Chicago, Álvarez met Ernest Lawrence, a physicist who won the Nobel Prize for his work on a machine that allows scientists to study the tiny particles that make up atoms. Everything around us, from the air we breathe to the food that we eat to the cells in our bodies, is made up of atoms.

Lawrence's machine meant that scientists could learn even more about the atoms that form everything in our world. Álvarez's sister Gladys had been working for Lawrence at his laboratory and introduced him to her brother. Lawrence was impressed by Álvarez's knowledge, great talent, and ambition, so he offered Álvarez a job at his laboratory, called the Berkeley Radiation Laboratory, in California. Álvarez accepted the job and moved to California with Geraldine, where he began his career as a researcher and professor.

Álvarez Learns from Others

After Álvarez moved to Berkeley and began working with Ernest Lawrence, he began to study **nuclear physics**. During this time, Álvarez read a lot, worked as a researcher, and went to weekly meetings with the other scientists at the lab. This group of scientists inspired his imagination and motivated his work. The scientists talked to Álvarez about his ideas and helped him to improve them. Their support was so important to Álvarez that he later continued the tradition, holding meetings in his home for his students.

Álvarez learned from scientists at Berkeley, but he also learned from scientists all over the world. He continued to read books and articles written by the best scientists in his field. Álvarez wanted to use the ideas and experiments of other scientists to make even greater discoveries. He admired their scientific achievements, but he also wanted take those achievements to new and exciting levels.

Early in his career, Álvarez worked with Dr. Ernest Lawrence, pictured here in 1938.

Álvarez is a great example of a successful scientist. He was a tremendous reader and experimenter, and most importantly, he questioned his own ideas, as well as those of others. Álvarez was never satisfied with his own ideas about new or even old scientific facts. Thinking carefully allowed him to see things in new ways. Because of his many ideas and his excitement about science and discoveries, Álvarez's **colleagues** gave him the nickname "Wild Idea Man."

This picture shows Álvarez at work in his lab at the University of California at Berkeley. Álvarez worked at Berkeley for more than twenty years.

Chapter 3:
A Scientist and a Teacher

Throughout his life, Álvarez made a lot of important discoveries and inventions. He was part of something called the era of "Big Science," a time when physicists were making lots of **breakthroughs**. Both governments and companies would use these discoveries. Some of them were related to atoms and the particles that form atoms, and they led to other discoveries and inventions that have changed the way that we look at the world and at science.

One of Álvarez's most important contributions to science was the **bubble chamber**, which he developed in 1954. Contrary to what you may be thinking, the bubble chamber has nothing to do with bubble gum or soap bubbles! It is a machine used to find and identify subatomic particles. Remember that subatomic particles are the tiny parts that make up atoms.

The Era of "Big Science"

During World War II, science entered into an era of what historians have called "Big Science." In this period, the U.S. government recognized that scientific research could lead to technologies useful to both the military and industry. It sponsored many scientific ideas with large amounts of money, causing the number of scientific research teachers, students, and facilities to grow. "Big Science" changed the nature of scientific research. Scientists began to require massive machines, budgets, and laboratories in order to test their theories and make new discoveries. The high costs made "Big Science" affordable only to government agencies, drawing influence away from the universities and individual sponsors that had been the main supporters of scientific research.

Álvarez discovered many other useful things. Some of his discoveries are used in binoculars, cameras, and televisions. He even designed a machine that helped President Eisenhower practice golf indoors! Nothing was too large or too small for Álvarez's imagination. He wanted to be the best in everything he did, including his hobbies.

It was not all studying or endless hours in the lab or library. Álvarez also held relaxed discussions at his home every week, as his mentor Ernest Lawrence had done before him. Both the friendship and challenging discussions at these meetings encouraged and expanded Álvarez's knowledge.

In this picture, a young Álvarez holds one of his many inventions.

Álvarez helped improve many useful things such as binoculars, cameras, and television.

In His Own Words

"People often say to me, 'I don't see how you can work in physics; it's so complicated and difficult.' But actually, physics is the simplest of all the sciences; it only seems difficult because physicists talk to each other in a language that most people don't understand—the language of mathematics. The thing that makes physics simple is that when we make a simple change in something, such as adding a little heat, we can easily predict that the whole thing is going to get warmer."

Álvarez enjoyed working hard, even at his hobbies. Flying, one of his favorite hobbies, requires physical strength and mental concentration. During his time off, Álvarez enjoyed beautiful views of the earth from high in the sky.

Álvarez also spoke of quiet times, hours of wondering and thinking. Early in his life, Álvarez's father advised him to "sit every few months in a reading chair for an entire evening, close your eyes, and try to think of new problems to solve." Álvarez took his father's advice very seriously and was glad that he did. His creative mind needed these quiet times as much as the time he spent actively exploring and concentrating on his work.

This picture shows an atomic bomb similar to the one dropped over Hiroshima, Japan during World War II. Álvarez played a key role in the invention of the atomic bomb.

Chapter 4:
The Dark Side of Discovery

In 1936, Álvarez worked as a researcher at the Lawrence Radiation Laboratory and was also a professor at the University of California at Berkeley. Álvarez's early years at Berkeley were active and productive. He and Ernest Lawrence were part of one of the best teams of physicists in the world.

In 1940, Álvarez moved from California to work at the Massachusetts Institute of Technology (MIT) in Cambridge, Massachusetts. MIT is one of the best schools of science, engineering, math, and technology. When Álvarez moved to MIT, it was a time when the government, the universities, and industry worked closely together. Álvarez went to MIT to work on inventions that would help the U.S. army during World War II.

When Álvarez began work at MIT, the United States was about to enter World War II. Then on the morning of December 7, 1941,

President Franklin D. Roosevelt signs the declaration of war against Japan.

Japan attacked the U.S. military bases at Pearl Harbor, located in Hawaii. More than 2,000 people lost their lives. The next day, President Franklin Roosevelt declared war against Japan.

When Álvarez started his job at MIT, he worked at a place called the "Radiation Laboratory," which developed radars and radios used by the army. The government gave it the name

World War II
1939–1945

World War II began in 1939, when the German army attacked Poland. By the time it was over in 1945, the war had involved nearly every part of the world. It was

called the "second world war" because there had been a first world war fought between 1914 and 1918. This war also involved many countries from different parts of the world.

In the 1930s, the leaders of Germany, Italy, and Japan were military dictators. They wanted to increase the size and power of their own nations at the expense of other countries. Many countries opposed them, like Great Britain, France, the Soviet Union, and the United States.

The United States entered the war in 1941 after the Japanese attacked Pearl Harbor in Hawaii. The war ended shortly after the United States dropped two atomic bombs on Japan in 1945. These bombs caused the worst destruction anyone had ever seen.

Between 35 and 60 million people died in the war. Some six million of those people were Jews. The German dictator, Adolf Hitler, and his Nazi Party tried to destroy the Jewish people.

"Radiation Lab" to hide its true purpose from other countries. Here, Álvarez worked on creating new radars. His group had the nickname "Luie's Gadgets," because of the many machines they created. Among other inventions, Álvarez developed a very good radar that was used to find targets on the ground. Even if a pilot could not see the target from the air, the radar helped him or her get much closer to the target.

Álvarez invented another important way to find targets using microwave technology, the same technology used by microwave ovens. This system allowed pilots to see other airplanes in the sky in heavy clouds, fog, and bad weather conditions. Another one of Álvarez's radars allowed airplane pilots to spot German submarines when they came to the ocean's surface. The system didn't just find the submarines. It "fooled" the submarine's detection system into not knowing how close the airplane really was. At the same time, as the aircraft became closer to the submarine, it received a stronger radar signal, allowing it to hit its target.

Álvarez Works with Enrico Fermi

Álvarez spent three years at MIT and then he returned to the University of Chicago in 1943. There he worked with Enrico Fermi, an Italian physicist who had come to the United States some years earlier. Fermi was the head of the Chicago section of what was called the **Manhattan Project**.

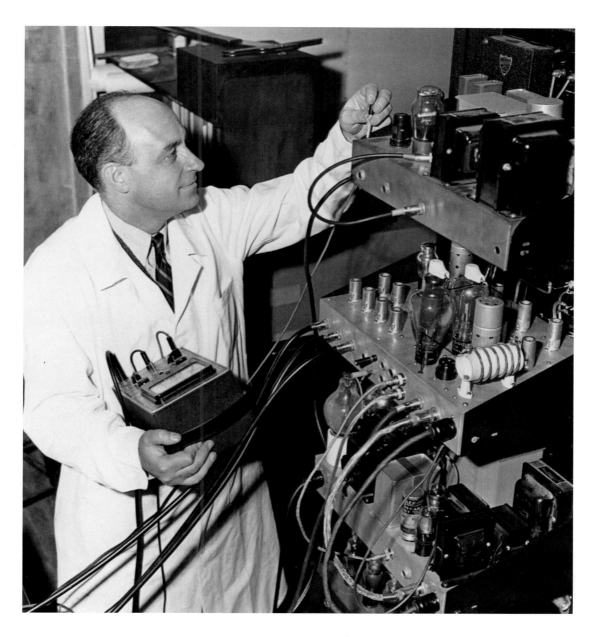

This is a photograph of Enrico Fermi, with whom Álvarez worked while at the University of Chicago.

The Manhattan Project

During World II, many scientists fled to the United States from Europe in order to escape the war. In 1939, three of those scientists, including Albert Einstein, wrote a letter to President Franklin D. Roosevelt. They warned him that scientists in Nazi Germany were working on the creation of nuclear weapons.

Roosevelt responded by setting up a committee to investigate the scientists' claims. By 1942, the U.S. government had created the Manhattan Project. Its goal was to create a nuclear weapon as quickly as possible. Scientists from all over the country were recruited by the U.S. government to produce an atomic bomb, a type of nuclear weapon.

The Manhattan Project involved many different research sites across the nation, but it mainly took place in three secret locations: Hanford, Washington; Los Alamos, New Mexico; and Oak Ridge, Tennessee. The existence of these sites was kept secret until the end of the war.

Part of the Los Alamos Laboratory.

Before World War II began, scientists in Germany had discovered one of the skills needed to create an atomic bomb. Concerned that the Germans would create an atomic bomb before the United States, Ernest Lawrence asked President Franklin Roosevelt to support the Manhattan Project. The program involved the research, testing, and production of the atomic bomb, and took place in different parts of the country, from Washington State to Oak Ridge, Tennessee.

By this time, Ernest Lawrence was a prominent physicist who had won the Nobel Prize for his work. He wanted to develop the atomic bomb, or at least keep ahead of the discoveries that German scientists were making. Because Álvarez had worked with him and knew a lot about subatomic particles, the government asked Álvarez and other important scientists to develop the atomic bomb. Since Lawrence had worked with Álvarez before, it is not surprising that Álvarez became an important member of the Manhattan Project.

At the University of Chicago, Fermi and Álvarez developed the first **nuclear reactor**, a device that controls the release of nuclear energy. Nuclear energy can be used to produce heat or electricity. It can also be used to set off an atomic weapon. One year after joining Fermi at the University of Chicago, Álvarez was moved to Los Alamos, New Mexico to work at the main headquarters for the Manhattan Project.

This photograph shows an aerial view of the Los Alamos National Laboratory, the main headquarters for the Manhattan Project.

Chapter 5:
The Los Alamos Lab Years

The war years were some of the most challenging of Álvarez's life. They were a time when his great ability to invent and to solve problems was needed for the goal of creating a weapon that would kill many people. These years were also hard because Álvarez was away from his wife and their children for long periods of time. He had to stay in a small apartment in the New Mexico desert. Like so many people during World War II, Álvarez and his wife felt the stress of war. Álvarez was away from home often, working on a secret project.

Under the direction of Robert Oppenheimer at the Los Alamos Lab, Álvarez and his colleagues worked hard to develop the first atomic bomb. Álvarez's job was important. He had to build a new type of **fuse**, a device that sets off the bomb. Álvarez's experience and knowledge of many scientific fields, from physics to electronics, helped him solve this problem.

Dr. Robert Oppenheimer (left) views the spot where the first atomic bomb was tested in July of 1945.

By 1945, scientists had successfully created three atomic bombs. After the bomb was developed, President Harry Truman wanted the war to be over as soon as possible, so he made the difficult decision to drop two atomic bombs on Japan. Many people were killed or injured. The bomb had very destructive effects on the land and the people where it was dropped.

The atomic bomb explodes over Nagasaki, Japan in 1945.

Álvarez saw the first explosion at the test site in New Mexico. When the bomb was dropped on Hiroshima, Japan, he rode in an airplane that followed the bomber and witnessed the destructive power of the bomb. He and his crew were shocked by the ruins they saw below them.

Even though Álvarez had seen the first bomb tested in the desert near Los Alamos, he did not realize until after the bombs were dropped in Japan that almost all of the people in those cities would die. Both the cities of Nagasaki and Hiroshima were destroyed, killing at least 100,000 people and many more over time. It would take years for each city to rebuild and recover from the effects of the bomb.

Despite his deep sadness over these deaths, Álvarez defended the bomb's use. He believed that if it had not been dropped, the war would have lasted longer, and even more people would have died. He also knew that more people had died from non-atomic bombs dropped on Japanese cities up until 1945 than in the two Japanese cities where the atomic bomb was dropped.

Álvarez did not have to fight in the war, but being a member of the Manhattan Project was not easy. It was difficult for him to see the destruction the bomb caused in Japan and know that he had been part of the team that caused it.

In this picture, a man observes the destruction after the bomb was dropped over Hiroshima, Japan. In front of him is a fireplace where a house once stood.

Since the bombing, people have discussed whether or not President Truman made the right decision. Some people think that using the atomic bomb was a good idea because they believe it helped end the war sooner. Others think that it was bad because it killed a lot of innocent people.

A surprise party was given for Álvarez in 1941 on his 25th anniversary with Berkeley National Lab.

Chapter 6:
Back to Berkeley

After the war ended, Álvarez returned to the University of California at Berkeley and became a professor of physics. He continued teaching for a long time, until he retired in 1978.

Back at Berkeley, Álvarez continued doing research. He was encouraged by the university's environment, which supported his creative work. At the time, subatomic particles were still a mystery, and Álvarez was determined to discover more about them. After he returned to teaching and working in the lab, Álvarez started developing devices to study the parts that form atoms. He built new machines that helped him develop the bubble chamber. This invention was so important that he was later awarded the Nobel Prize for it.

Álvarez knew that in order to understand subatomic particles better, he would need to invent new machines. So he worked hard to improve the machines scientists were already using. Ernest Lawrence continued to guide Álvarez and many of the men who had worked on the Los Alamos project. He was ready to help them when they needed his knowledge and experience to solve the difficult problems on which each scientist worked.

The Lawrence Team

While Álvarez went back to teaching at the university after the war, he also kept working with Lawrence's team. He felt that Lawrence was a wonderful scientist and teacher. Álvarez liked working with him because Lawrence trusted everyone on his team. Lawrence also encouraged each scientist to be independent. Álvarez enjoyed this environment, where he could work with others while continuing with his own projects.

Álvarez said that the lab was a great place to learn and discover. Scientific knowledge grew, and the scientists grew as people. They explored new ideas, learned from each other, and kept trying, even if they made mistakes and things did not work out as they had planned.

Álvarez was a very successful inventor and a great scientist, but his inventions and discoveries took a lot of hard work. Breakthroughs do not just happen overnight. They come only after months and even years of effort. But hard work and patience pay off, as we can see from Álvarez's example. He not only made a lot

Álvarez and His Research Teams

When Álvarez worked on the bubble chamber and other machines, he used the help of his research assistants. A research assistant is a student who helps a more experienced scientist do experiments. When Álvarez received the Nobel Prize for the bubble chamber, he thanked the scientists at the Lawrence Lab and at Berkeley who worked with him for many years.

Álvarez's achievements show the importance of working as a team. Some of the most important discoveries in science are made thanks to many people working together to solve a problem.

Paul Hernandez, Dr. Edwin McMillan, Dr. Luis Álvarez, and Don Gow stand next to the bubble chamber.

Álvarez stands with a bubble chamber display that was built at Berkeley.

of important discoveries and inventions, but his work was appreciated by the government and universities.

Álvarez also worked as a **consultant**, or an advisor, for different companies. Many companies wanted him to teach them about the inventions he had worked on and how to use those inventions in everyday life. For more than ten years, he worked as a consultant at the same time that he was working as a teacher.

Álvarez was also involved in a project to design satellites to orbit Earth. He was part of a team of MIT researchers who worked on this project years before the Soviet Union launched *Sputnik* in the 1950s. *Sputnik* was the first satellite ever to be put into space.

All of this interesting work kept Álvarez's creative mind busy and happy. When Álvarez found a problem that seemed to have no solution, he looked for new ways of tackling the problem until he discovered a way to solve it.

Awards and Honors

After Álvarez finished his work on the bubble chamber and other devices, he was accepted into the National Academy of Sciences in 1947. The National Academy of Sciences is an organization that accepts only the best scientists, and it is a great honor to belong to it. That same year, Álvarez also received an award from President Truman in a ceremony at the White House!

Here, Álvarez shakes hands with President Harry Truman.

Álvarez won many awards and honors for his inventions and discoveries. The most important of these was the Nobel Prize, which he won in 1968. When Álvarez won the Nobel Prize, one of his colleagues said, "Practically all the discoveries that have been made in the important field of **particle physics** have been possible only through the use of methods developed by Professor Álvarez." That's not something they would say about just anyone! Álvarez was deeply touched and honored.

Even though he received many honors and awards, Álvarez was a humble man. During his entire life, his main goal was to continue learning about the many things that interested him. He also tried to learn more from his research, his colleagues, and his students. In all of his years teaching and working in the lab, Álvarez never lost sight of the importance of working with other people to become a great scientist.

Álvarez was recognized for his inventive work when he received the Nobel Prize, the highest honor any scientist can achieve. In this photograph, Álvarez speaks at the Nobel Prize ceremony on October 12, 1968.

Chapter 7:
Inventions and Theories

After World War II, many countries, especially the United States and Russia, competed with one another to see who could build the strongest bomb. After Russia exploded its first nuclear bomb in 1949, the U.S. government became more and more interested in developing a more powerful kind of bomb, called "the Super."

Ernest Lawrence also thought it was a good idea to build more powerful bombs. Álvarez wasn't sure about developing even more destructive weapons, but he also believed that if the United States and Russia had the same number and the same kind of weapons, this would keep them from starting a nuclear war that could destroy both nations.

So in the 1950s, Álvarez did more research on subatomic particles. As he discovered new particles, he was driven to discover more about the parts of the atom. Scientists used to believe that atoms were the smallest units that make up everything in the world. Today, we know that atoms are formed by even smaller units of matter. These ideas would not exist today had it not been for the efforts of people such as Luis Álvarez.

Álvarez wanted to develop devices that allowed scientists to study subatomic particles better. That is how he ended up developing the bubble chamber in 1954. As you have read, the bubble chamber was a machine used to find and identify subatomic particles, the tiny parts that make up atoms.

A New Beginning

In the midst of Álvarez's successful work as a scientist, he went through difficult times in his personal life. Álvarez and his wife had been married for 21 years, but Álvarez spent so much time away from home that they ended up not feeling close to each other any more. In the end, they decided to get divorced.

Soon, however, Álvarez found new love. In 1958, he married Jan, a lab assistant with lots of training in science. They were both in love with science, which was one of the reasons they felt so connected to one another. For the rest of his life, Jan was Álvarez's friend and scientific inspiration. Even when she did not participate directly in his research, she understood it and encouraged him. She was both a colleague and a loving wife. They eventually started their own family and had two children, Helen and Donald.

1958 was also a sad year for Álvarez because his dear friend Ernest Lawrence died. For many years, Lawrence had been a very important person in Álvarez's life, teaching him, working with him, and always pushing him to do his best. It was a very difficult loss for Álvarez.

The Nobel Prize

In 1968, Álvarez was awarded the Nobel Prize for his contributions to physics, particularly for the bubble chamber that he had developed. This was a very important honor for him, since the Nobel Prize is the top recognition any scientist can hope for. But that certainly didn't mean he stopped working! In the following years, Álvarez continued to work at Berkeley, and he was also asked by the government and various companies to do more consulting work.

Álvarez's work took him in many different directions. One time, he helped the government study the camera footage that was taken when President John F. Kennedy was shot and killed in Dallas, Texas. On another assignment, he went to Egypt to examine one of the pyramids at Giza to find out if there were any hidden rooms (he and his team concluded that there were none). Álvarez also worked with optics, his first love in college, and developed lenses that were later used in binoculars and cameras. His knowledge as an inventor was as amazing as his discoveries in modern physics.

The Nobel Prize

In the early 1900s, the Swedish inventor Alfred Nobel decided to use his fortune for the good of all people. Nobel had invented dynamite, and he wanted to ensure that important inventors, scientists, and artists received the support that they would need in order to achieve their goals. He made sure that, after his death, prizes would be given to people who had managed to do important things to improve our world.

Nobel created a prize for various categories. Great writers would get the Nobel Prize for Literature, people who had done things for world peace would get the Nobel Peace Prize, and scientists who had made important discoveries would get the Nobel Prizes for Physics, **Chemistry**, and Medicine. Even world leaders, such as former U.S. President Jimmy Carter, have received the Nobel Prize.

More than 100 years later, Nobel prizes are still awarded each year. Apart from the honor of receiving the prize, winners get a gold medal and a large amount of money. Since Alfred Nobel was Swedish, the Nobel Prize ceremony takes place in Stockholm, the capital of Sweden. The King of Sweden gives out the prizes at this very impressive event.

In this photograph, Álvarez (right) receives the Nobel Prize Award for Physics from King Gustav VI of Sweden.

In His Own Words

When he accepted his Nobel Prize, Álvarez said:

"I am very happy that a number of my young colleagues are here tonight to share with me this prize that we have been awarded thanks to our joint efforts over the years. The Nobel Prize is given to just one person, rather than to a group, but we all understand that our work really was a group effort."

In 1978, ten years after winning the Nobel Prize, Álvarez retired from his position as director of the Lawrence Lab and stopped teaching at the University of California at Berkeley.

Father and Son

After Álvarez retired from teaching and research, he began another adventure, this time with his son, Dr. Walter Álvarez, who had become a geologist. Together, he and Walter searched for the reasons that dinosaurs had become extinct. Their ideas were based on evidence that asteroids or meteors may have crashed into the earth millions of years ago. Álvarez and Walter thought that the meteors hit the earth so hard that they changed the climate, causing the dinosaurs to die.

Walter, the geologist, and Luis, the physicist, began to discuss the earth. Walter knew a lot about geology and what the earth is made of. Álvarez was an expert in physics. By combining their knowledge, they were able to come up with a new theory.

Their theory was called "the impact theory of extinction," and it explained why dinosaurs, which had ruled the earth for more than 100 million years, suddenly died out. Álvarez and Walter discussed many issues related to the dinosaurs, such as how they lived and what the earth looked like when they existed.

Luis Álvarez and Walter Álvarez stand with colleagues above a nuclear reactor in 1985. Later in his life, Álvarez and his son hunted for geological clues to prove that a giant asteroid hit the earth 91 million years ago.

Álvarez and his son worked to learn more about the life and death of the dinosaurs and why their environment suddenly changed. They started by studying rocks in Italy. They discovered a layer of rock that contained a high level of a rare metal. This layer was sandwiched between rocks from around 65 million years ago. In 1980, Álvarez and his son published an article about this discovery. In their article, they said that they believed the metal came from an asteroid that hit the earth millions of years ago. According to their theory, this explosion caused the sun's light to be blocked out and led to the extinction of the dinosaurs.

Álvarez and Walter knew that a huge impact must have taken place millions of years ago. Other scientists were also thinking that meteor impacts could explain why there are giant craters on Earth, such as one called Chicxulub, in Mexico. Many people think that the crater was formed when a huge meteor hit Earth, causing the death of the dinosaurs and other creatures. They believe that when the meteor hit, it caused a storm of fire that covered much of the North American continent. All life in that area burned up.

Álvarez thought that the impact caused darkness around the world. The debris from the impact, combined with the smoke from the fires, might have filled Earth's atmosphere like dense clouds. No sunlight could get through the thick, dirty blanket. Plants stopped growing. Plant-eating animals starved, and then animals that eat other animals starved as well.

Álvarez and Walter worked together on an expedition in Italy in 1987.

Álvarez and Walter's theory about dinosaur extinction, which agreed with the other scientists' ideas about the Mexican crater, is now accepted by many as one of the best theories to explain the death of the dinosaurs. In this way, Álvarez was able to make an important contribution to the science of geology, even though it wasn't an area of science that he had previously studied.

Álvarez always kept his mind open and made his life a learning experience. He died of cancer in 1988, but he left behind many important discoveries, inventions, and theories. And he always remembered to enjoy everything he did.

Luis Walter Álvarez's life is an example of how hard work leads to great achievements. In this photograph, Álvarez receives congratulatory phone calls after the Nobel Prize Award is announced.

Glossary

atomic bomb highly destructive bomb that is a type of nuclear weapon

atoms basic building blocks of matter; they make up all objects

aviation use of airplanes and other aircraft

breakthrough sudden advance in knowledge or science

bubble chamber device used to find and identify subatomic particles

chemistry study of chemical substances and the changes that take place when they combine with one another

colleague person who works with another in a professional setting

consultant person who gives professional advice to others

diverse coming from many different cultures

extinct plant or animal that has died off

fuse device that sets off, or detonates, a bomb

geologist person who studies geology, the science that deals with the history of the earth and its life, especially as recorded in rocks

Manhattan Project secret U.S. government project to develop the atomic bomb during World War II

Nobel Prize award given each year for outstanding achievement in physics, chemistry, medicine, literature, peace, and economics

nuclear physics science that deals with the particles that form the nucleus of an atom

nuclear reactor device used for the controlled release of nuclear energy, which can be used to produce heat or electricity

nuclear weapon type of weapon that has enormous destructive power; nuclear weapons have only been used in one war, when the United States dropped the atomic bomb on two Japanese cities during World War II

optics branch of physics that deals with light, lenses, and vision

particle physics branch of physics related to parts of matter smaller than the atom

physics study of physical objects and the way they are moved by energy

researcher person who studies and does experiments to learn new things in a certain subject

resourceful able to think of ways, or means, to do something

Timeline

June 13, 1911 Luis Walter Álvarez is born in San Francisco, California.

1928 Graduates from Rochester High School and begins studies at the University of Chicago.

1932 Receives B.S. degree from the University of Chicago.

1934 Receives M.S. degree from the University of Chicago.

1936 Receives Ph.D. from the University of Chicago; marries Geraldine, his first wife; accepts research position with Ernest Lawrence at Lawrence Radiation Laboratory; becomes assistant professor at the University of California at Berkeley.

1940 Moves to Massachusetts Institute of Technology to work on radar and other systems for the military.

1944 Moves to Los Alamos, New Mexico, to work on the Manhattan Project.

1945 Rides in plane behind the *Enola Gay* when it dropped the bomb on Hiroshima.

1945 Returns to University of California at Berkeley, where he is made a full professor; continues work at the Lawrence Radiation Laboratory.

1954 Develops the bubble chamber.

1958 After having divorced his first wife, Álvarez marries Jan.

1968 Awarded the Nobel Prize.

1973 Visits Italy and investigates the extinction of dinosaurs with his son Walter.

1978 Retires from faculty at the University of California at Berkeley and from the Lawrence Lab.

1988 Dies of cancer.

Further Information

Further Reading

Goldstein, Natalie. *How Do We Know the Nature of the Atom?* New York: The Rosen Publishing Group, 2001.

Nardo, Don. *Atoms*. Farmington Hills, MI: Gale Group, 2001.

St. John, Jetty. *Hispanic Scientists*. Bloomington, MN: Capstone Press, 1996.

Addresses

National Academy of Sciences
500 Fifth Street, N.W.
Washington, DC 20001

National Museum of Nuclear Science and History
1905 Mountain Road N.W.
Albuquerque, NM 87104

Index